for Congreg...

EVERLASTING
PRAISE

3

Arranged by

MIKE SPECK &
STAN WHITMIRE

Orchestrated by

WAYNE HAUN &
CHRIS MCDONALD

PUBLISHING COMPANY

MIKE SPECK
MUSIC

lillenas.com

NO SWEETER NAME

includes
O How I Love Jesus
No Sweeter Name
Jesus, Name Above All Names
Take the Name of Jesus with You

Arr. by Mike Spec
and Stan Whitmir

For medleys following the tracks, perform the endings marked with asterisks.

O How I Love Jesus

FREDERICK WHITFIELD

TRADITIONAL AMERICAN MELODY
Arr. by Mike Spec
and Stan Whitmir

Do Not Photocopy

No Sweeter Name

Words and Music by
KARI JOBE
Arr. by Mike Speck
and Stan Whitmire

dark - ness a-round me. You are the hope_____ to the

hope - less and bro - ken. You are the on - ly

CD 1:3

Song ending

*Medley ending

truth and the way._____

Jesus, Name Above All Names

Words and Music by
NAIDA HEARN
*Arr. by Mike Speck
and Stan Whitmire*

♩. = ca. 66
Unison

mf

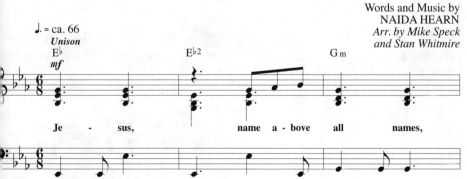

Je - sus, name a - bove all names,

6

Take the Name of Jesus with You

DIA BAXTER

WILLIAM H. DOANE
Arr. by Mike Speck
and Stan Whitmire

You are the life___ to my heart and my soul. You are the light___ to the dark - ness a - round me. You are the hope___ to the hope - less and bro - ken. You are the on - ly

10

TODAY IS THE DAY

includes
Today Is the Day
Leaning on the Everlasting Arms
I Know Who Holds Tomorrow

*Arr. by Mike Speck
and Stan Whitmire*

For medleys following the tracks, perform the endings marked with asterisks.

Today Is the Day

Words and Music by
LINCOLN BREWSTER
and PAUL BALOCHE
*Arr. by Mike Speck
and Stan Whitmire*

To-day is the day___ You___ have made;___ I will re-joice_

To-day is the day.

To - day is the day_____ You__ have made;

I will re - joice_____ and be glad__ in__ it.

To - day is the day_____ You__ have made,

I will re - joice_____ and be glad__ in___ it._____

And I_____ won't wor - ry a -

bout to - mor - row, I'm trust - ing in what___ You say._____

To - day is the day._____

Leaning on the Everlasting Arms

ELISHA A. HOFFMAN

ANTHONY J. SHOWALTER
*Arr. by Mike Speck
and Stan Whitmire*

I Know Who Holds Tomorrow

Words and Music b
IRA F. STANPHILL
Arr. by Mike Spee
and Stan Whitmi

20

MY SAVIOR LIVES

includes
Easter Song
My Savior Lives
He Lives
He's Alive

Arr. by Mike Speck
and Stan Whitmire

For medleys following the tracks, perform the endings marked with asterisks.

Easter Song

Words and Music by
ANNE HERRING
Arr. by Mike Speck
and Stan Whitmire

22

23

24

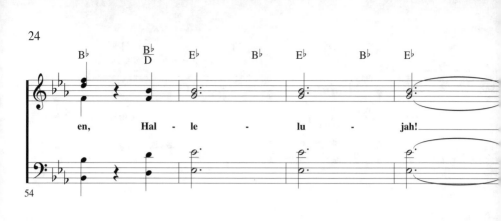

en, Hal - le - lu - jah!

54

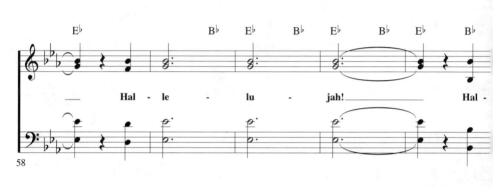

Hal - le - lu - jah! Hal -

58

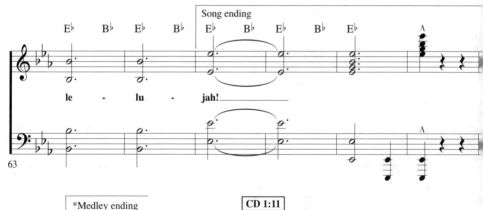

Song ending

le - lu - jah!

63

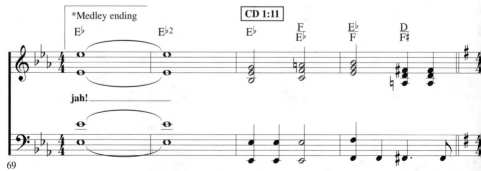

*Medley ending

CD 1:11

jah!

My Savior Lives

Words and Music by
JON EGAN
and GLENN PACKIAM
*Arr. by Mike Speck
and Stan Whitmire*

I know that my Re - deem - er lives, and now I stand on what He did. My Sav - ior, my Sav - ior lives.

Ev - 'ry day a brand new chance to say, "Je - sus, You are the on - ly way."

26

My Sav - ior, my Sav - ior lives!

CD 1:12

The King has come____ from heav-en and dark - ness trem -

- bles at His name.____ Vic - to - ry____ for - ev - er

G 2(no3)   **E**m7(4)

Ev-'ry day a brand___ new chance___ to say,____ "Je - sus, You are___

Em7(4)   **C** 2(no3)

___ the on - ly way."____ My Sav - ior,

CD 1:13

C 2(no3)   Song ending **G**   *Medley ending **G**

my Sav - ior lives!

He Lives

Words and Music by
ALFRED H. ACKLEY
Arr. by Mike Speck
and Stan Whitmire

♩ = 138

C D C/E D/F♯ *Unison* G   E♭7/C♯5   C M7

He lives, He lives! Christ Je - sus lives___ to

30

He's Alive

Words and Music by
DON FRANCISCO
Arr. by Mike Speck
and Stan Whitmire

UNFETTERED PRAISE

includes
Excellent Lord
Joyful, Joyful, We Adore Thee

*Arr. by Mike Speck
and Stan Whitmire*

For medleys following the tracks, perform the endings marked with asterisks.

Excellent Lord

Words and Music by
TREMAINE HAWKINS
and **MYIIA DAVIS HAWKINS**
*Arr. by Mike Speck
and Stan Whitmire*

You are my God, You are my King. Ex - cel - lent Lord, be ex -
alt - ed on high. Un - fet - tered praise, to You will I sing.

34

Ex - cel - lent Lord, be ex - alt - ed on high. alt - ed on high.

Hal - le - lu - jah, Hal - le - lu - jah,

Hal - le - lu - jah! Ex - cel - lent Lord, be ex - alt - ed on high.

Joyful, Joyful, We Adore Thee

HENRY VAN DYKE

LUDWIG VAN BEETHOVE
Arr. by Mike Spe
and Stan Whitm

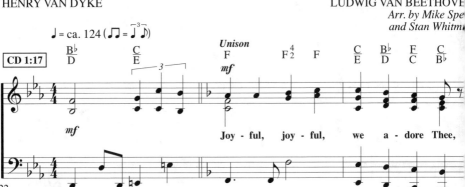

Joy - ful, joy - ful, we a - dore Thee,

36

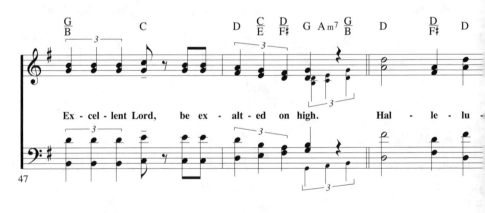

37

THROUGH THE STORM

includes
He Hideth My Soul
Still
Made Me Glad
I Need Thee Every Hour

Arr. by Mike Spe
and Stan Whitmi

For medleys following the tracks, perform the endings marked with asterisks.

He Hideth My Soul

FANNY J. CROSBY

WILLIAM J. KIRKPATRIC
Arr. by Mike Spe
and Stan Whitmi

40

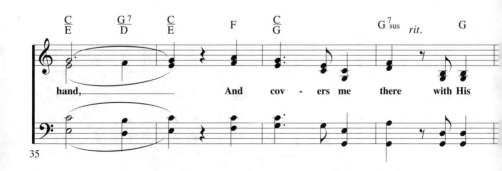

Still

Words and Music by
REUBEN MORGAN
*Arr. by Mike Speck
and Stan Whitmire*

Hide me now un- der Your wings.____ Cov - er me____ with-

Made Me Glad

Words and Music by
MIRIAM WEBSTER
Arr. by Mike Speck
and Stan Whitmire

♩ = ca. 81

CD 1:22

Parts

Fa-ther, You are King o-ver the flood; I will be still

and know You are God.

And I will not be moved

and I'll say of the Lord: You are my Shield,

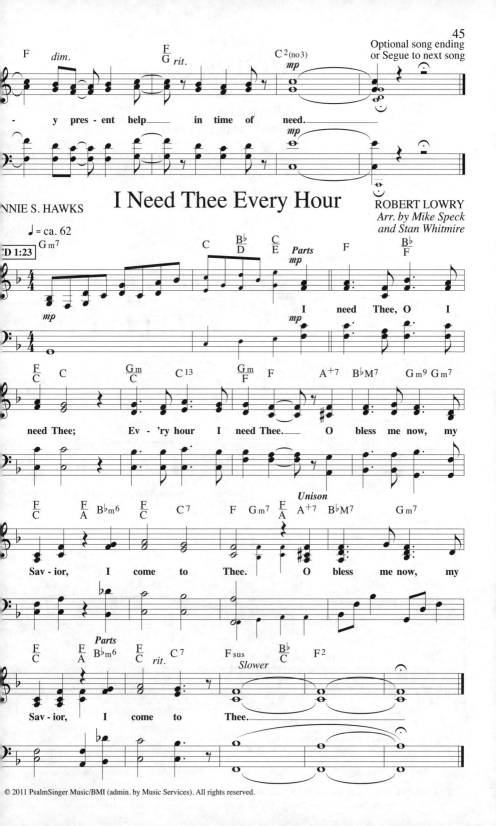

I Need Thee Every Hour

ANNIE S. HAWKS

ROBERT LOWRY
*Arr. by Mike Speck
and Stan Whitmire*

REVIVE US

includes
Revive Us Again
We Need to Hear from You

Arr. by Mike Spe
and Stan Whitmi

For medleys following the tracks, perform the endings marked with asterisks.

Revive Us Again

WILLIAM P. MACKAY

Words and Music |
JOHN J. HUSBAN
Arr. by Mike Spe
and Stan Whitm

Do Not
Photocoμ

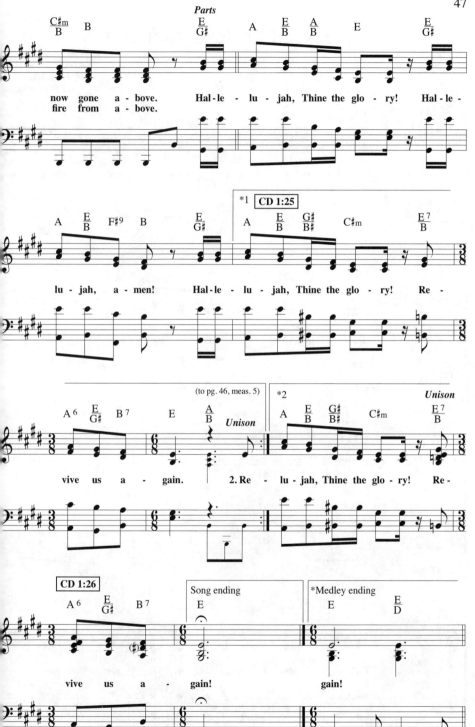

We Need to Hear from You

Words and Music b[y]
SANDRA CROUC[H]
Arr. by Mike Spe[e]
and Stan Whitmi[re]

♪ = ca. 120 (swing 16ths)

We need to hear from You, We need a word from You; If we don't hear from You what will we do? Want-ing You more each day to show us Your per - fect

CD 1:27

way. There is no oth - er way___ that we can live.___

SOLO freely

De-struc - tion is___ now, is now___ in

view. Seems the world has for-got-ten all a-bout You.___

Saints have stopped cry - ing and Your church - es are

Dm Gm7 $\frac{F}{C}$ B♭

38

dy - ing;___ we're so lost with - out You.___

$\frac{F}{A}$ Dm7 E♭ $\frac{E♭}{D♭}$

40

You said if we'd___ seek,___ if we'd seek___ Your

$\frac{B♭}{C}$ C $\frac{B♭}{D}$ $\frac{C}{E}$ F A7

42

EVERLASTING GOD

includes
A Mighty Fortress Is Our God
Everlasting God
Total Praise

Arr. by Mike Speck
and Stan Whitmire

For medleys following the tracks, perform the endings marked with asterisks.

A Mighty Fortress Is Our God

Words and Music by
MARTN LUTHER
Arr. by Mike Speck
and Stan Whitmire

CD 1:28

♩ = ca. 104

A might-y for-tress is our God, a bul-wark nev-er fail - ing; Our

54

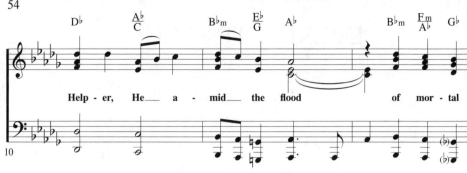

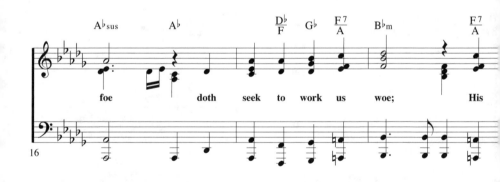

Everlasting God

Words and Music by
BRENTON BROWN
and KEN RILEY
*Arr. by Mike Speck
and Stan Whitmire*

56

58

ea - gles._____ You are____ the ev - er - last - ing God,

the ev - er - last - ing God;_____ You do___

__ not faint,__ You____ won't, grow wear - y.____

You're the___ de - fend - er of___ the weak,_____ You com

- fort those___ in need,_____ You lift___ us up___ on

Total Praise

Words and Music by
RICHARD SMALLWOOD
*Arr. by Mike Speck
and Stan Whitmire*

60

WITH ALL MY HEART

includes
With All My Heart
The Name of the Lord
Holy, Holy, Holy!
All Hail King Jesus

*Arr. by Mike Spe(
and Stan Whitmi(*

For medleys following the tracks, perform the endings marked with asterisks.

With All My Heart

Words and Music b
MORRIS CHAPMA
and BILL BATSTON
*Arr. Mike Spe(
and Stan Whitmi(*

Medley Sequence copyright © 2011 by PsalmSinger Music/BMI (admin. by Music Services). All rights reserved.

PLEASE NOTE: Copying of this product is NOT covered by CCLI licenses. For CCLI information call 1-800-234-2446.

The Name of the Lord

Words and Music by
CLINTON UTTERBACH
*Arr. Mike Speck
and Stan Whitmire*

Holy, Holy, Holy!

REGINALD HEBER

JOHN B. DYKE
Arr. Mike Spe
and Stan Whitmi

68

All Hail King Jesus

Words and Music by
DAVE MOOD
Arr. Mike Spec
and Stan Whitmi

70

WHAT A SAVIOR

includes
Hallelujah! What a Savior
O What a Savior

Arr. by Mike Speck
and Stan Whitmire

For medleys following the tracks, perform the endings marked with asterisks.

Hallelujah! What a Savior

Words and Music by
PHILIP P. BLISS
Arr. by Mike Speck
and Stan Whitmire

PLEASE NOTE: Copying of this product is NOT covered by CCLI licenses. For CCLI information call 1-800-234-2446.

72

O What a Savior

Words and Music
MARVIN P. DALTO
*Arr. by Mike Spe
and Stan Whitm*

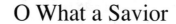

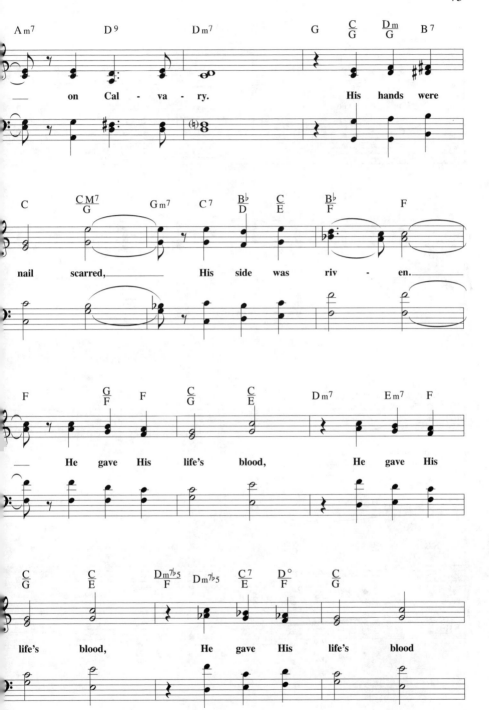

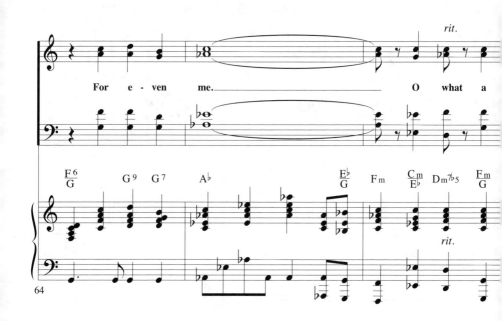

WE WILL REMEMBER

Words and Music by
TOMMY WALKER
*Arr. by Mike Speck
and Stan Whitmire*

Lyrics:

1. We will re-mem-ber, we will re-mem-ber, we will re-mem-ber the works of Your hands.

We will stop and give You praise for

Medley Sequence copyright © 2011 by PsalmSinger Music/BMI (admin. by Music Services). All rights reserved.

78

80

CD 1:46

82

We will re - mem - ber, we will re - mem - ber,

we will re - mem - ber the works of Your hands.

We will stop and give You praise for

great is Thy faith - ful - ness.

mp

We will re - mem - ber,   we will re - mem - ber,

we will re - mem - ber   the works of Your hands.

We will stop and give You praise for

great is Thy faith - ful - ness.

We will re - mem - ber, we will re - mem - ber,

87

we will re - mem - ber the works of Your hands.

89

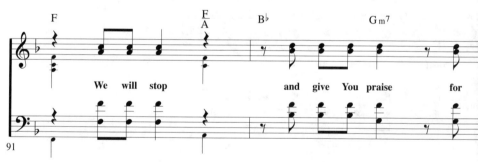

We will stop and give You praise for

91

great is Thy faith - ful - ness. Thy faith - ful - ness.

93

SUSTAINING GRACE

includes
Great Is Thy Faithfulness
Your Grace Is Enough
More than Enough

*Arr. by Mike Speck
and Stan Whitmire*

For medleys following the tracks, perform the endings marked with asterisks.

Great Is Thy Faithfulness

THOMAS O. CHISHOLM

WILLIAM M. RUNYAN
*Arr. by Mike Speck
and Stan Whitmire*

see; All I have need - ed Thy

hand hath pro - vid - ed. Great is Thy

Song ending

*Medley ending

faith - ful - ness, Lord un - to me. me.

Your Grace Is Enough

Words and Music by
MATT MAHER
*Arr. by Mike Speck
and Stan Whitmire*

CD 1:51

1. Great is___ Your faith-
2. Great is___ Your love___

(to pg. 91, meas. 45

grace is e-nough_____ for _____ me.

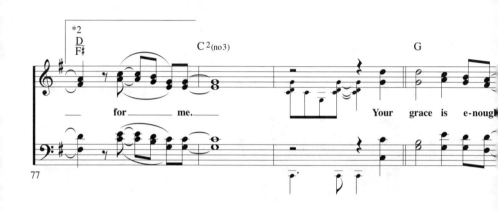

____ for _____ me._____ Your grace is e-noug

Your grace is e-nough,_____ Your grace is e-noug

Optional song endi
or Segue to next so

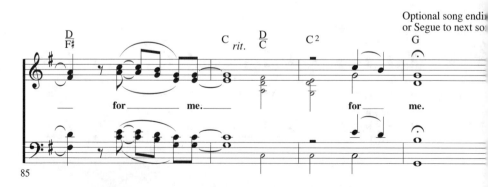

_____ for _____ me._____ for _____ me.

More than Enough

Words and Music by
ROBERT GRAY
*Arr. by Mike Speck
and Stan Whitmire*

96

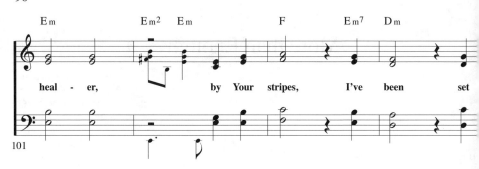

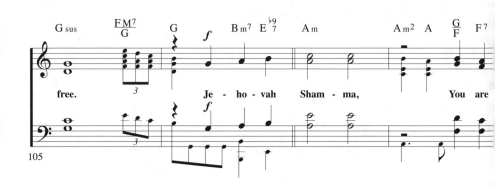

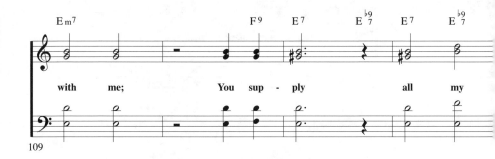

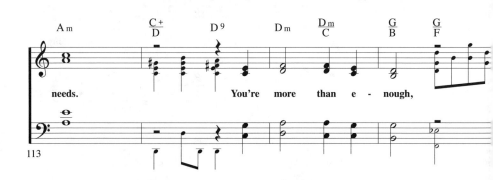

SING, SING, SING

includes
Sing, Sing, Sing
Lord, I Lift Your Name on High
This Is the Time I Must Sing

Arr. by Mike Spe...
and Stan Whitmi...

For medleys following the tracks, perform the endings marked with asterisks.

Sing, Sing, Sing

Words and Music
JESSE REEVES, DANIEL CARSO...
CHRIS TOMLIN, TRAVIS NUN...
and MATT GILDE...
Arr. by Mike Spe...
and Stan Whitmi...

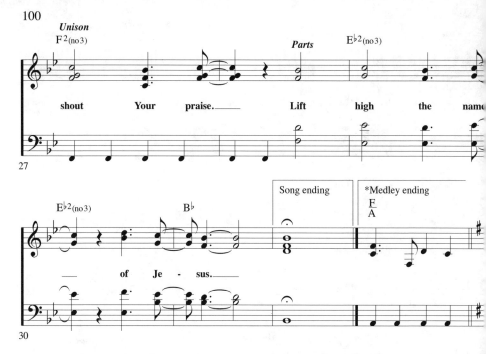

Lord, I Lift Your Name on High

Words and Music
RICK FOUNI
Arr. by Mike Spe
and Stan Whitm

from the earth___ to the cross___ my debt___ to pay.

46

From the cross___ to the grave,___ from the grave___ to the sky

48

(to pg. 101, meas. 44)

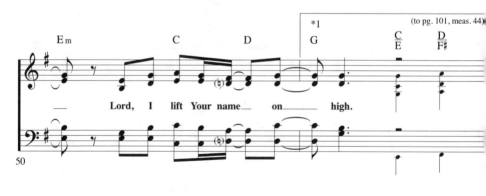

___ Lord, I lift Your name___ on___ high.

50

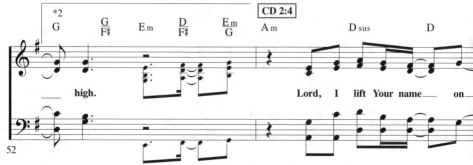

___ high. Lord, I lift Your name___ on

52

CD 2:4

high the name of Je-sus.

This Is the Time I Must Sing

WILLIAM J. GAITHER
and GLORIA GAITHER

WILLIAM J. GAITHE
Arr. by Mike Spe
and Stan Whitmi

si - lent, ye moun - tains, ye fields and ye foun - tains, for

this is the time I must sing._____ It's the

JESUS MESSIAH

includes
Jesus Messiah
All Hail the Power of Jesus' Name
Stronger

Arr. by Mike Spe(
and Stan Whitmi(

For medleys following the tracks, perform the endings marked with asterisks.

Jesus Messiah

Words and Music k
CHRIS TOMLIN, DANIEL CARSON
JESSE REEVES and ED CAS
Arr. by Mike Spe(
and Stan Whitmi(

He be-came sin who knew no sin that

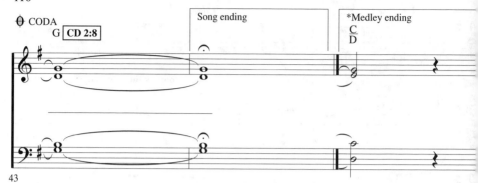

All Hail the Power of Jesus' Name

EDWARD PERRONET

OLIVER HOLDE

Arr. by Mike Spe
and Stan Whitmi

112

Stronger

Words and Music by
REUBEN MORGAN
and BEN FIELDING
*Arr. by Mike Speck
and Stan Whitmire*

114

LIVING HE LOVED ME

includes
Since Jesus Came into My Heart
One Day
Victory in Jesus
Love Lifted Me

*Arr. by Mike Speck
and Stan Whitmire*

For medleys following the tracks, perform the endings marked with asterisks.

Since Jesus Came into My Heart

RUFUS H. McDANIEL

CHARLES H. GABRIEL
*Arr. by Mike Speck
and Stan Whitmire*

What a won-der-ful change in my life has been wrought since

116

118

One Day

CHARLES H. MARS
Arr. by Mike Spe
and Stan Whitmi

♩ = ca. 117

Liv - ing He loved me, dy - ing He saved me,

bur - ied He car - ried my sins far a - way;

Ris - ing He jus - ti - fied free - ly, for - ev - er:

CD 2:13 *2nd time*

One day He's com - ing back, O glo - ri - ous

day!   day!

(to pg. 118, meas. 23)

Victory in Jesus

Words and Music by
EUGENE M. BARTLETT
*Arr. by Mike Speck
and Stan Whitmire*

♩ = ca. 117

Unison

O vic - to - ry in Je - sus, my

120

122

Ris - ing He jus - ti - fied   free - ly,___ for - ev - er:___

A♭   A♭/C   D♭   D°7

53

CD 2:14

One day___ He's com - ing back, O glo - ri - ous

A♭   E°   Fm   D♭m/F♭   A♭/E♭   E♭7

55

Song ending   *Medley ending

day!   day!

Song ending   *Medley ending

A♭   E

57

Love Lifted Me

JAMES ROWE

HOWARD E. SMITH
Arr. by Mike Speck
and Stan Whitmire

Love lift - ed me, Love lift - ed

me. _____ When noth - ing else could help

Love lift - ed me. Love lift - ed

me, Love lift - ed me.

124

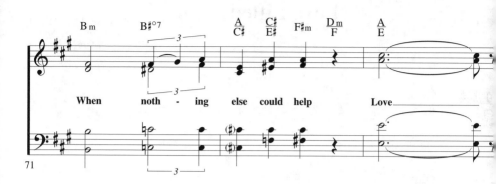

When noth - ing else could help Love

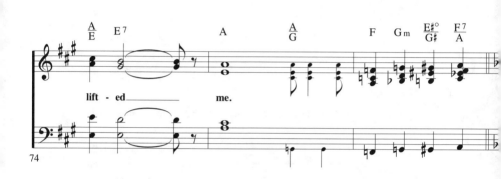

lift - ed me.

Liv - ing He loved me, dy - ing He saved me,

126

Liv - ing He loved___ me, dy - ing He saved___ me,

B♭7   A♭7   A7   B♭7   A♭7   A7

85

bur - ied He car - ried my sins far___ a - way;___

B♭7   C7   F   F7/A

87

Ris - ing He jus - ti - fied free - ly,___ for - ev - er:___

B♭   B♭/D   E♭   E°7

89

AT THE CROSS

includes
Down at the Cross
At the Cross
I Will Glory in the Cross

Arr. by Mike Spe
and Stan Whitmi

For medleys following the tracks, perform the endings marked with asterisks.

Down at the Cross

ELISHA A. HOFFMAN

JOHN H. STOCKTO
Arr. by Mike Spe
and Stan Whitmi

Down at the cross, where my Sav - ior died;

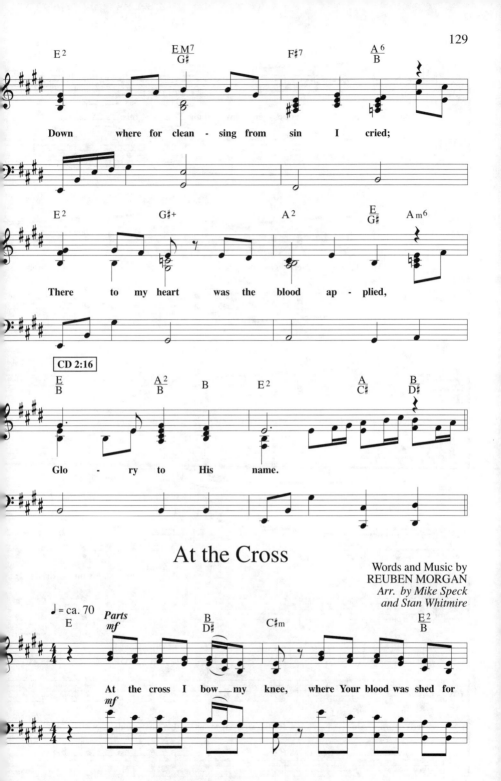

Down where for clean - sing from sin I cried;

There to my heart was the blood ap - plied,

CD 2:16

Glo - ry to His name.

At the Cross

Words and Music by
REUBEN MORGAN
*Arr. by Mike Speck
and Stan Whitmire*

♩ = ca. 70

Parts

At the cross I bow my knee, where Your blood was shed for

130

There at the cross where He took me in; Glory to His name. At the cross I bow my knee, where Your blood was shed for me, there's no greater love than this. You have overcome the grave, Your glory fills the highest place, What can separate me

I Will Glory in the Cross

Words and Music b
DOTTIE RAMB
Arr. by Mike Spe
and Stan Whitmi

FOR ALL YOU'VE DONE

includes
For All You've Done
All Because of Jesus
My Tribute
Thank You, Lord

Arr. by Mike Spec
and Stan Whitmi

For medleys following the tracks, perform the endings marked with asterisks.

For All You've Done

Words and Music t
REUBEN MORGA
Arr. by Mike Spec
and Stan Whitmi

138

All Because of Jesus

Words and Music
STEVE FI
Arr. by Mike Spe
and Stan Whitm

140

that cov-ers me,___ and raised this dead___ man's life_____ and it's all___ be-cause___ of Je - sus, I'm___ a-live.___ And it's all_____ be-cause___ of Je - sus, I'm___ a-live.

My Tribute

Words and Music by
ANDRAÉ CROUCH
*Arr. by Mike Speck
and Stan Whitmire*

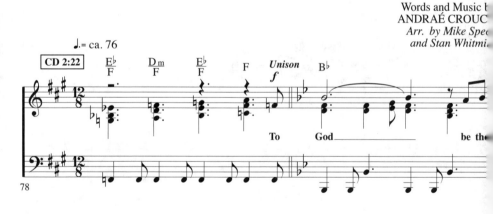

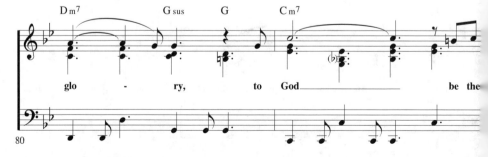

Thank You, Lord

Words and Music b
DENNIS JERNIGA
Arr. by Mike Spec
and Stan Whitmi

THE BLOOD OF JESUS

includes

There Is a Fountain
O the Blood
Nothing but the Blood

Arr. by Mike Speck
and Stan Whitmire

For medleys following the tracks, perform the endings marked with asterisks.

There Is a Fountain

WILLIAM COWPER

TRADITIONAL AMERICAN MELODY
Arr. by Mike Speck
and Stan Whitmire

There— is a foun - tain filled with blood drawn—

Do Not
Photocopy

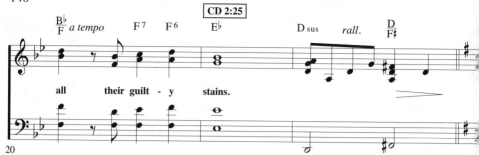

O the Blood

Words and Music by
MARY ELIZABETH MILLER
and THOMAS MILLER
*Arr. by Mike Speck
and Stan Whitmire*

149

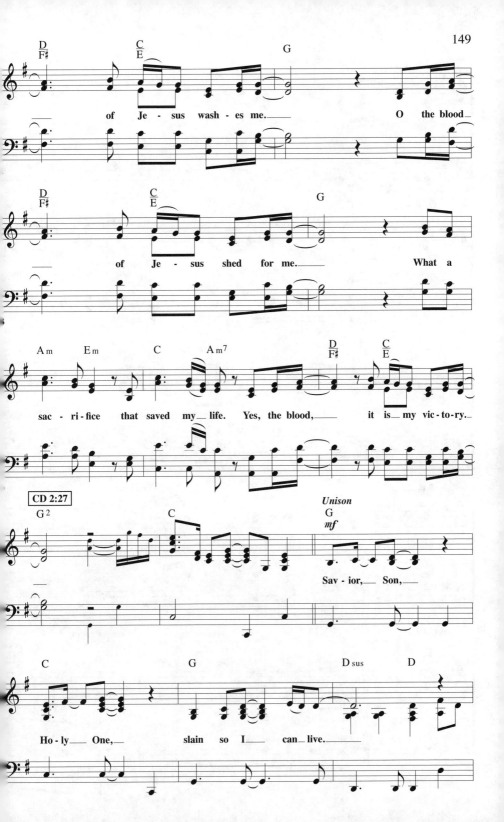

of Je - sus wash - es me.____ O the blood____

of Je - sus shed for me.____ What a

sac - ri - fice that saved my__ life. Yes, the blood,____ it is__ my vic - to - ry.____

CD 2:27

Unison

Sav - ior,__ Son,__

Ho - ly__ One,__ slain so I__ can__ live.____

150

See the Lamb, the great I AM, Who takes a-way my sin. O the blood of Je - sus wash - es me. O the blood of Je - sus shed for me. What a sac - ri - fice that saved my life. Yes, the blood, it is my vic - to - ry.

CD 2:28

Song ending

*Medley ending

Nothing but the Blood

Words and Music by
ROBERT LOWRY
*Arr. by Mike Speck
and Stan Whitmire*

JESUS, OUR ROCK

includes

God Is My Refuge and Strength
I Go to the Rock

*Arr. by Mike Speck
and Stan Whitmire*

For medleys following the tracks, perform the endings marked with asterisks.

God Is My Refuge and Strength

Words and Music by
MICHAEL POPHAM
*Arr. by Mike Speck
and Stan Whitmire*

154

156

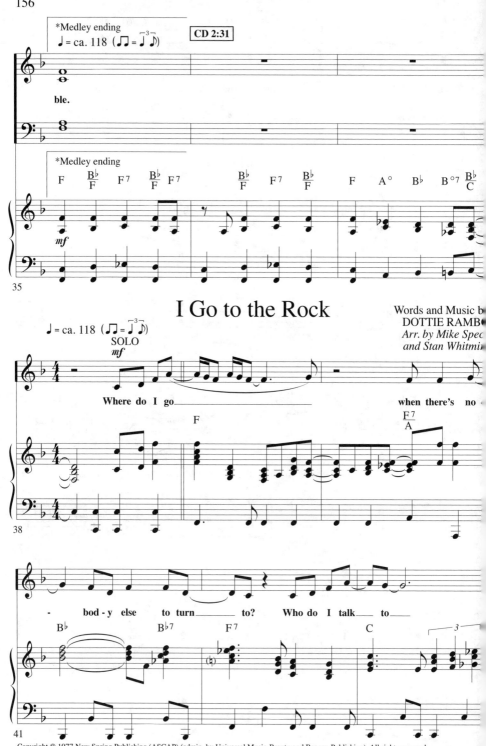

I Go to the Rock

Words and Music by
DOTTIE RAMBO
Arr. by Mike Speck
and Stan Whitmire

158

OUR GOD IS GREAT

includes
How Great Is Our God
Our God
Our God Reigns

Arr. by Mike Spe(
and Stan Whitmi

For medleys following the tracks, perform the endings marked with asterisks.

How Great Is Our God

Words and Music
CHRIS TOMLIN, JESSE REEVE
and ED CAS
Arr. by Mike Spe
and Stan Whitmi

The splen - dor of___ the King,___

clothed in maj - es - ty,___ let all the earth___ re - joice.

Do Not
Photoco

166

Our God

Words and Music by
**JESSE REEVES, CHRIS TOMLIN,
MATT REDMAN and JONAS MYRIN**
*Arr. by Mike Speck
and Stan Whitmire*

Our God Reigns

Words and Music b
LEONARD E. SMIT
Arr. by Mike Spe
and Stan Whitmi

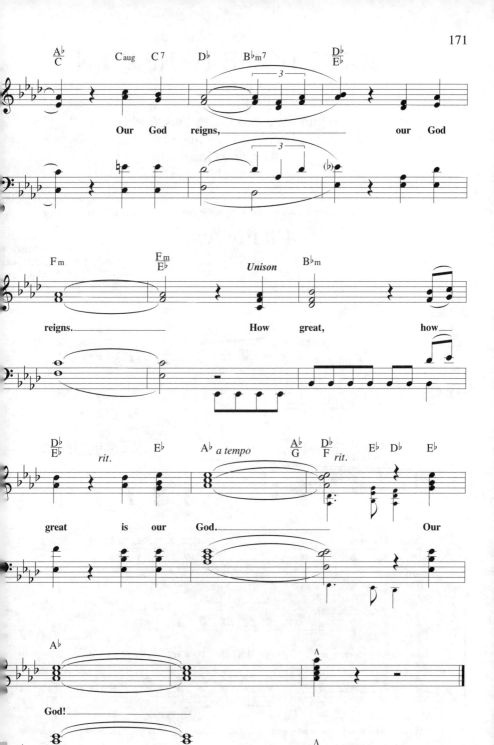

GOING HOME TO HEAVEN

includes
I'll Fly Away
Gettin' Ready to Leave This World
I Feel like Traveling On
Amazing Grace
Going Home

Arr. by Mike Spe
and Stan Whitmi

For medleys following the tracks, perform the endings marked with asterisks.

I'll Fly Away

Words and Music b
ALBERT E. BRUMLE
Arr. by Mike Spe
and Stan Whitmi

Some glad morn-ing when this life is o'er,_____ I'll_____ fly

Do Not
Photoco

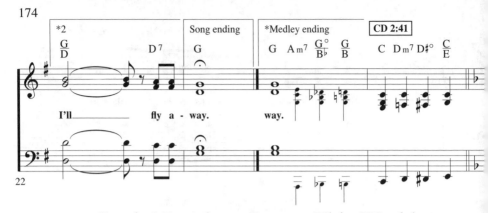

Gettin' Ready to Leave This World

Words and Music
LUTHER G. PRESLE
Arr. by Mike Spe
and Stan Whitm

I Feel like Traveling On

WILLIAM HUNTER

ANONYMOUS
*Arr. by Mike Speck
and Stan Whitmire*

♩ = ca. 89 *(swing sixteenths)*

I feel like trav-el-ing, trav-el-ing on. I feel like trav-el-ing trav-el-ing on. My heav-en-ly home is bright and fair, I feel like trav-el-ing on; My heav-en-ly home is bright and fair, I feel like trav-el-ing

Amazing Grace

JOHN NEWTON

"Virginia Harmony
Arr. by Mike Spe
and Stan Whitmi

safe ___ thus ___ far, and grace will ___ lead me

CD 2:44

a tempo, a little slower

home. ___

Going Home

WILLIAM J. GAITHER
and GLORIA GAITHER

WILLIAM J. GAITHER
Arr. by Mike Speck
and Stan Whitmire

Go - ing home, I'm go - ing ___ home, there is

178

I WILL RISE

Words and Music by
LOUIE GIGLIO, CHRIS TOMLIN,
MATT MAHER and JESSE REEVES
*Arr. by Mike Speck
and Stan Whitmire*

$\sharp$ = ca. 84

CD 2:45

1. There's a peace I've come to know,_____ though my

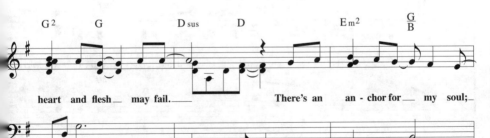

heart and flesh__ may fail._____ There's an an-chor for__ my soul;

more pain. I will rise, on ea - gle's wings; be - fore

my God, fall on my knees and rise,

I will rise.

2. There's a

day that's draw - ing near when this

dark - ness breaks to light; and the shad - ows dis - ap - pear,

184

Topical Index
Song and MEDLEY Titles

ASSURANCE & TRUST
Everlasting God, 55
God Is My Refuge and Strength, 153
He Hideth My Soul, 38
I Go to the Rock, 156
I Know Who Holds Tomorrow, 18
I Need Thee Every Hour, 45
JESUS, OUR ROCK, 153
Leaning on the Everlasting Arms, 15
Still, 41
TODAY IS THE DAY, 11
Today Is the Day, 11

ATTRIBUTES OF GOD
A Mighty Fortress Is Our God, 53
EVERLASTING GOD, 53
Everlasting God, 55
God Is My Refuge and Strength, 153
Great Is Thy Faithfulness, 89
How Great Is Our God, 162
Jesus Messiah, 106
JESUS, OUR ROCK, 153
Made Me Glad, 43
Our God, 167
OUR GOD IS GREAT, 162
THROUGH THE STORM, 38
We Will Remember, 77
WITH ALL OF MY HEART, 62
Your Grace Is Enough, 91

BLOOD OF CHRIST
At the Cross, 129
Down at the Cross, 128
My Tribute, 142
Nothing but the Blood, 151
O the Blood, 148
THE BLOOD OF JESUS, 146
There Is a Fountain, 146

CALL TO PRAISE
SING, SING, SING, 98

COMFORT & PEACE
God Is My Refuge and Strength, 153
Great Is Thy Faithfulness, 89
He Hideth My Soul, 38
I Go to the Rock, 156
I Will Rise, 179
Leaning on the Everlasting Arms, 15
Still, 41
THROUGH THE STORM, 38
We Will Remember, 77

CONSECRATION
I Need Thee Every Hour, 45

**ETERNAL LIFE &
    SECOND COMING**
All Hail King Jesus, 68
Gettin' Ready to Leave This World,
    174
Going Home, 177
GOING HOME TO HEAVEN, 172
Hallelujah! What a Savior, 71
I Feel like Traveling On, 175
I Will Rise, 179
I'll Fly Away, 172
LIVING HE LOVED ME, 115
One Day, 118

GOD'S LOVE
At the Cross, 129
He Hideth My Soul, 38
Love Lifted Me, 123

GRACE
Amazing Grace, 176
SUSTAINING GRACE, 89
Your Grace Is Enough, 91

JESUS CHRIST—LORDSHIP
All Hail King Jesus, 68
All Hail the Power of Jesus' Name,
    110
Excellent Lord, 33

Medley Index

Alphabetical Index

Song and **MEDLEY** Titles